Contents

G000123767

To my parents Brighid and Jack.

Davoren Hanna was born in Dublin in 1975. His poetry has received The Christy Brown Award, The British Spastics Society National Literary Award and won the Welsh Academy Young Writers' Competition and The Observer National Children's Poetry Competition. The story of his life is told in Poised for Flight, the R.T.E. documentary. This is his first book.

NOT
COMMON
SPEECH

the voice
of
Davoren
Hanna

Raven Arts Press/Dublin

NOT COMMON SPEECH
is first published in Dublin by
THE RAVEN ARTS PRESS
P.O. Box 1430
Finglas
Dublin 11
Ireland.

ISBN 1 85186 076 2

Acknowledgements

The publishers would like to thank John Carlos of *The Sunday Tribune* (front cover) and Brian Farrell of *The Irish Independent* and John Rowley of *The Irish Press* (back cover) for permission to use their photographs.

The author would like to acknowledge that certain of these poems have already appeared in *Die Horen* (Translated by Peter Jankowsky), The Connacht Tribune, RTE, BBC, the anthology entitled *How the Earth was formed Quiz,* and *Letter to a Friend* (Puffin Books).

The title of this book is taken from *A Common Ground* by Denise Levertov.

Designed by Dermot Bolger & Aidan Murphy. Cover design by Susanne Linde. Printed and bound in Ireland by Colour Books Ltd., Baldoyle.

INTRODUCTION

The notion that Davoren Hanna was once considered "retarded" will seem incredible to those who read this book of moving and memorable poems. But he was, in fact, so considered; and the impulse of much of his poetry is a joyous cry of delight at discovering that his genius has finally been discovered though its full potential has yet to be realised. His mother and father are to be thanked for this; and Davoren thanks them in the inimitable Davoren way.

Most people in prison are able to express what it actually means to be imprisoned. For seven years, Davoren was locked in the prison of himself. A key made of love unlocked him. But during those seven years a fair amount of rage and frustration had built up in his heart. Anybody who reads this book looking for sentimental verse should simply not bother to open it; there is anger here, real, elemental fury; there is frustration and nightmare and isolation; and there is a superb intelligence combined with a vigilant, generous heart to produce poems that people will read again and again for their human music and verbal skill.

When a poet is as isolated as Davoren has been, and to some extent still is, he tends to have an understanding of feelings and states of mind which are in profound opposition and yet are deeply connected with each other. So Davoren writes with searing insight about loneliness, as in *Birth Hidden From an Uncaring World* or *Gethsemane;* but he responds with joyous appreciation to scenes of triumphant togetherness acclaiming athletic prowess, as in *Freewheeling Champ.* All through this collection there is a sense of opposition at work: stagnation and movement, dumbness and eloquence, the crippled individual and the energy, at once brutal and beautiful, of the world, the images of being ignored and neglected jostling with images of being observed and acclaimed. Running through all these oppositions, harnessing them and making them coherent in well-crafted poems, is the intense energy of a complex, articulate psyche which has both a developed sense of tragedy and a rascally sense of humour. I believe this comic side of Davoren will emerge more and more.

7

Make no mistake about this: Davoren Hanna is a fine poet and a bit of a rascal. If he weren't a bit of a rascal he wouldn't be the magnificent spirit he is. And I know perfectly well that the poet and the rascal combine to produce a fragile, vulnerable, heroic figure who, released from his humiliating, terrifying, enraging prison of misunderstood isolation, is now enriching all our lives with poems that in themselves are reasons for celebration and gratitude.

Brendan Kennelly,
Dublin,
1989.

NOTES FROM *A BONE FRAGMENT* — FLESHED OUT WITH POEMS.

Born light years ago during a storm of Lot's wife's making, womb-silenced, I lived wordlessly as an apparently retarded child. Then at seven years of age I said my first word — Mama. It was spelt out in red plastic letters on a black magnetic board. Never had a word been beaten into shape like that one.

Limbs as sclerotic as mine have little or no voluntary movement. When you think of Christy Brown you think of feet. My feet are ice-fettered inside boots of lead. When you think of Christopher Nolan you see head-cupped unicorns tumbling among meadows of mellifluous words. But I can't even hold up my head or point with my eyes, so limp is my body at times.

When those who doubt the authenticity of my voice ask how can a boy like that possibly communicate with such severe physical handicap, a satanic fury overcomes me. Long have I turned on the relentless roasting spit of logic. When will I convince these people that my poems are my voice, not anybody else's? My voice has been totally camouflaged by silent vocal chords. It is not merely muffled. It cannot be accessed through speech therapy. A brain scan taken when I was five years old showed an abnormality consistent with severe physical disability. My brain's ability to signal my distress at being intellectually undermined did not register on the C.A.T. scan.

Can you imagine being trapped inside a burning building not knowing that the fire brigade couldn't hear your cries because the noise of breaking glass and crashing timber filled their ears? I inhaled the noxious fumes of platitudes, misunderstanding and misdiagnosis during my early years.

The sun had disappeared from my sky. Not believing what the logical negativists had diagnosed, my parents

9

homerically nurtured me with music, stories and moments of splendid madness. In their rational mood, they too engaged in doubting Thomas fact-searching before they fully believed I was intellectually unimpaired.

My life until I went to school at nine had been spent listening to adult conversations. I held conversations in my head but nobody heard them. Being mainly limited to my home during my early days helped me to develop powers of deep concentration such that I listened not just with my ears but with my heart. I heard not only conversations on a wide range of topics but I also plunged, delved and scavenged inside other people's heads. Whispers of thought increased to mighty clamours of insight and I grew "wise beyond my years".

My first word was my greatest achievement — my Everest. I have jumped more gullies and scaled more peaks since that day, but that word Mama fumblingly pushed with folded fist across the black meadow of magnetic board liberated me from an eternity of nothingness. Bright red was the word, bright gold were the tears of relief in my heart! My jubilation lit the skies.

Words define my world as feet define the dancer's. Portentous poems flowed from my dammed-up stream. But unfortunately I only baffled the experts more by using big words and rich concepts considered more suited to an adult than a handicapped child. When asked at nine why I wrote poetry, I answered "Orzinary communicashyon is too slow to zucsincly indeecat my meaning." As doubt grew, great despair engulfed me when I realised that I could continue to spend my life seemingly retarded while inside very bright. Poetry became my life-line.

This collection contains a sample of some of my best poems. I have numerous other poems, some private, some incomplete, and some not yet put on paper because I type using my bum. My mother, father, friends and helpers hold me notwithstanding the pressure of my bony bottom on

10

their knees, so that I can touch the keys with my fisted hand. There have been many other poems of unprintable quality due to my mother censoring them. You can guess what mothers most disapprove of and imagine the rest!

Life is grim for many handicapped children in this country. Spending time despairing instead of playing is not normal for children. Growing up indoors all the days of our childhood is not normal either. My most lonely days were spent in centres and schools for mentally retarded and physically disabled children. *Gethsemane* was my garden. *Half Loaves* were not enough to stave off my hunger for wholeness and raw self-doubt seared my soul. Out of barren soil grew the daunted *Sapling* asking why? whither? wherefore? Yet soil that is barren can be watered and look what harvest can result. Love had seen fit to shower down on my patch.

Never having had the love of brothers and sisters, I had a solitary childhood but my world was peopled with wonderful adult friends like Cian and Annette whose influence on my work has been enormous (*Firebirds* and *Annette*). They never doubted me. Listening to their encouraging comments, I responded by working harder at my poems. I don't live the life of an average handicapped child because I have had lots of dangerous adventures like climbing mountains with Cian, my head in the clouds, my heart in my ecstatic mouth.

The heart-in-mouth exhilaration of my first real canoe trip was sensational not only because I was flung into dangerous rapids but because freedom from my muscle-tightening mother (much as I love her) was really liberating (*Tom Sawyer, Eat Your Heart Out*). Wanting friends of my own age, I sought to go to my local national school. St Patrick's Boys National School was game to have me. My classmates were lads with big hearts and bold faces who accepted me for the brat that I was. My favourite subject geography resonated with my questioning restless soul (*Geographic Landmarks*). Summer exam became a

Darwinian refutation through Socratic dialogue with my brilliant and witty teacher Eoin Shanahan (*How the Earth Was Formed Quiz*).

I love history but, having seen *Holocaust* on TV, plummeting spirits caused me to doubt an almighty God who could let millions of Jews be exterminated. I had great difficulty making my confirmation at 12 but I made it instead one year later, my faith renewed through the music of Messiaen, who survived to praise God despite having been in a concentration camp.

My father played a huge part in my artistic development and an even greater role in my spiritual life (*Falcon*). Can a father forgive a son who sought to give him cheeky advice on how how to find truth, when the father in question is the epitome of true fatherly love, the kind God gives to his ungrateful rascally children?

Though suffering is easier to write about , I've included poems of triumph and happiness. I've had moments of glory winning several poetry competitions. My hero, Stephen Roche, and I cycled to win, both having overcome falling from our saddles (*Freewheeling Champ*). In my case it was failure to convince the sceptics that I had a separate existence from that of my mother. My other hero, Christy Brown and I have one thing in common, mothers who listened intuitively to their mute crippled sons and who gave them a chance to dance down all the days of their lives. To Christy and to all my silent friends I dedicate *Seas Damned Shall Take the Arid Earth by Storm*.

I sing now every day especially when my inventive saviours, David Vernon and Jim Davenport, come to my house and open my voice-box with their magic keys. To these two men, to Peter Jankowsky, Barry Gleeson and Brendan Kennelly, and to all who have helped me, especially June Levine, I dedicate *Lines in Times of Great Happiness*.

TWO FOXY SCRIBES
(For Ted Hughes)

Silver-silent I —
golden-tailed you —
we both tell time-riddles.

Limping across
snow-scarred moonscapes,
the spheres tumble at our bark.

FAMINE

Woven banks of weeds
pay their last respects
to rank potato stalks —
now razed and ravaged
by hungry folk.
Lamentation purples
the tepid wind,
tinging it with dolour.
Tormented corpses fill
the maw of the famine crucible.
A small boy stands still —
astounded to be there.

HOLOCAUST

Only hell can have been more horrific
as lines of skeletal angels fell
from the grace of one called Hitler.
Grimly gesturing towards the steady throng,
the sentinel of death allocated chambers.
Sepia ran the earth with the blood
of the sons and daughters of Zion.
Weep, o weep, all you who love humanity.

HOW THE EARTH WAS FORMED QUIZ

What does a volcano do?
It sends Pliny the Roman naturalist
rushing to Vesuvius's gaping jaw
in search of its scarlet secret.
And how was the earth's crust formed?
Heaven's master-baker,
Lord of holocausts and light,
touched his dough with fingers of fire
and then sighed upon it.
And do lines of latitude run north to south?
Why, a swallows's heart-quickening
will tell the way home to his haven
whatever way the lines are drawn.

SEAS DAMNED SHALL TAKE THE ARID EARTH BY STORM
(In memory of Christy Brown)

Feet were made for walking
But not yours — the hell they weren't!
Sun poured through your kinked toes
Whenever the hungry paint licked your soul.
Down all the dancing days of your life,
When incoherence fought with grey uncertainty,
You longed for calloused-handed truth.
Living vibrantly in song and tales of youth,
The dammed up seas of resonance
Shall take the arid earth by storm.

FREEWHEELING CHAMP

I listened to the roar
of victory in my ears.
Inch by painful inch
I rode with him —
plummeting downhill,
swerving, gliding,
rising with his wry
Dublin humour
rolling in my spokes.
Satin ribbon roads
slipped under my wheels,
but undaunted came I
to vanquish all doubt
riding in triumph
onto the Champs Elyseés.

TOM SAWYER, EAT YOUR HEART OUT!

I grimaced in pain.
Freed from my bonds
of muscle-tightening mother stricture,
I worshipped at the shrine of boyhood.
The light was Burmese — brown
on the brackish river.
The frail craft bobbed wildly
on the swirling water.
It made torrential queasy womenfolk
faint with fear at our intrepidity.
Each rapid overcame,
we plunged over the precipice
of questioning adolescence,
leaving Huckleberry Finn
to row back to the shore.

I ASK BUT FOR THE DIVINER'S WAND

Pleats, stumps, loam —
words like these are clay-bound.
When I search for glimmering sounds
I scan the skies hoping
to harvest love-knots.
Ploughing the depths,
I turn up the bedrock clay.
I home into water
but waste such precious hours
treasure-hunting the juicy soil.
A sally rod twitches —
water stirs in the gathered
folds of the earth's petticoat —
would that I too had the diviner's wand.

FIREBIRDS
To Cian

We are insurrection survivors.
Rising when the ashes have cooled,
we spread our tremulous wings.
Reeling from the acrid smoke of burnt dreams,
we soar — none the worse for having scattered
great illusory schemes into fragments
which float mirthlessly in the glowing sky.
Going lustily into battle we had little to lose,
now we have myriad flight-paths to travel together.

TRAWLER

To my friend Paul,
on his thirteenth birthday.

Lost in thought,
the little round-eyed cabin boy
gazed into seascapes of dappled grey.
Light trawled the salt-troubled sea
in search of pain-free answers.
When he heard his captain call,
he donned his woolly hat and stood at the helm.
Waves sang a mournful song in his attentive ear.
As tortured sailors loudly cursed their lot,
watch was declared. Hour by white hour went by.
From the depths of barnacled fears
he tugged at manhood's line.
Stout was his fisted tug.

GETHSEMANE

Sentenced, punished, parodied —
we live in a grey habitat
as light denies us hope.
The great garden blooms anew
but no purpose have we here
fixed like stakes to the budding rose
nay, riveted to Christ's calvary-tree.

LIFT THE EDGES
(For Barry)

Licked by salt-silvered streams of unshed tears,
my cheeks crave grief-channels where agony can lie.
Selfish sorrows need not linger long
since they nick but few notches in my sapling bark.
Grief bites into my bole and lodges in knots
of silent gall, dulling my raging soul.
Green furrows, lift your edges and valley my tears.

DEATH OF A SPACE SHUTTLE

The pinnacle of fame, lightning-struck.
Perhaps round-shouldered Atlas grew weary
and dropped his orb upon their frail craft?
Salvage, O salvage their dreams, Lord,
as you enfold them in your vast canopy.

They did not leave deep treatises
on the meaning of the universe.
No, theirs was a greater legacy —
a waltz among the stars with death's armament
freely spinning in a sunless shrieking sky.

THE DANCING BEAR

Festivities will never stop at Berlin's wall.
Streets that were once lugubrious grey
now entangle as lovers do through
the long-limbed summer nights.
Seeking admission to the nuptial feast,
flesh once striped by searchlight-beams
now dances arm in arm with comrades
on the other side of freedom's wall.
Slow caravans of eager immigrants
bring knapsacked hopes in their hearts.
Light kindles the naked callous stones
and luminous dreams mutate the skies.

November 1989

GEOGRAPHIC LANDMARKS

The best of all subjects is geography!
Fearsome distances disappear into coloured
shapes like felt-animal jigsaws.
Rivers wriggle like inky worms
across the sellotaped pages of my atlas.
Lakes and mountains nudge each other
sideways as they fight for space
upon my topsy-turvy sandwiched map.
Would Gulliver step on little towns
if the world was as small as this?
Quiet spaces surround me as I ponder,
wide prairies await me when I wander.

BIRTH HIDDEN FROM FROM AN UNCARING WORLD

He came forth
breech-birthed.

Stars wept
when they heard
the Virgin scream
and blood filled the sky.

Safe delivery hurried,
Joseph cut the grief-cord.
He lies severed now
from her frail flesh.

Child reddened
by history's blood sacrifice,
do you ever ask yourself
why me?

MY LIFE, MY VOICE, MY STORY

The moon blackened at my birth
and long night's cry began.
Pain became my bed-fellow
and despair my song.
God disappeared behind the clouds;
I lost my star-signpost to hope.

Light found a chink to peep through
when poems were read to my starved soul.
Loneliness brought moments of repose;
lines poured through my veins
and love glimmered on my tongue.
Little birds became my inspiration.

Left with my own silent melody,
I painted notes of long-forgotten tunes
trembling in my trapped heart.
Light burst through my dark mouth
and myriad songs flew heavenwards.
I was poised for flight...

ANNETTE

Tiny grains of fine sand
trouble the oyster in his shell,
yet look what rich harvest comes forth.
Touched by your gentle beauty,
my solitary seed grows luminous
and bursts its constraining bonds.

SAPLING BENT BY A CRUEL WIND

Awful asymmetry;
wheeled and twisted children —
love's foolhardy moment
soldered into frail flesh —
tacitly I watch them
slide into oblivion
as their dreams freeze
in the bitter barren air.
Who has ordained it so?
By what legerdemain
did such lamentation
befall the innocent?
When almost all creatures
beget their kind,
whither our benighted tribe?

HALF LOAVES
(First Communion)

The bells pealed loudly
as children pinioned
by chair and calipers
limped or wheeled into church.

Poignant scenes awaited
gathering onlookers
while photographers
froze the spectacle in time.

Timidly mothers smiled
trying to look inconspicuous
as public eyes gazed
in naked curiosity.

The priest obliged
with goblet of wine
but I wanted to taste
the loaf of suffering.

Pictures show my smile
but my hunger bit deep;
loneliness helmeted my heart
in case it broke.

Weep not, birds,
in song though I am mute,
my spirit sings with you
in praise of our maker.

FALCON

Plummeting into grey,
the falcon swerved
to touch the water
as time took a breath.
I heard his cry
and saw the glint of hope
in his grieving feathers.
Father, you grow wise
in your search for truth.
But real truth remains
hidden behind the grin
you wear in childhood photographs
still fixed limply
to dry reason's wall.
Soar, father, soar.

LINES IN TIMES OF GREAT HAPPINESS

Ploughman, you can never know
the pleasure of seafaring
straddled as you are
across the earth's brown back.
Were I to sail upon the crest
of happiness surging in my heart
clay thoughts would crumble
and my harrowed tongue be freed.